P9-CAS-300

SCHOLASTIC

BEST PRACTICES *in Action*

Partner Poems for Building Fluency

by Bobbi Katz

New York • Toronto • London • Auckland • Sydney

Mexico City • New Delhi • Hong Kong • Buenos Aires

Teaching *Resources*

For two cheerleaders for poetry,
Bernice Cullinan
and
Lee Bennett Hopkins

Scholastic Inc. grants teachers permission to photocopy the poems from this book for classroom use. No other part of this publication may be reproduced in whole or in part, or stored in a retrieval system, or transmitted in any form or by any means, electronic, mechanical, photocopying, recording, or otherwise, without written permission of the publisher. For information regarding permission, write to Scholastic Inc., 557 Broadway, New York, NY 10012-3999.

Cover design by Brian LaRossa
Interior design by Diana Fitter
Interior illustrations by Diana Fitter, Mike Gordon, Anne Kennedy, and Mike Moran
Teaching activities by Pamela Chanko.
ISBN–13: 978-0-439-55437-4
ISBN–10: 0-439-55437-3
Poems copyright © 2001 and 2007 by Bobbi Katz.
Teaching activities copyright © 2007 by Scholastic, Inc.

Published by Scholastic Inc.
All rights reserved.
Printed in the U.S.A.

5 6 7 8 9 10   40   13 12 11 10

Contents

Lessons & Poems

Introduction

As teachers, we know how important it is to help students become fluent readers. Once students learn to read a text accurately and quickly, they are able to focus on its meaning. Mastering fluency helps make language every student's friend: the friend they can depend on to gather information, voice ideas, and express emotions. As students build fluency skills, they also make important connections between written and spoken language. Fluent reading involves expressive speaking and attentive listening. How can we give students the whole-language experiences they need to build essential fluency skills? With *Partner Poems for Building Fluency*, you'll see that fluency can indeed be taught through direct, explicit instruction. And what's more, it can be fun!

The poems in this book can help students build fluency through active engagement in reading, speaking, and listening, as they experience the delight of language. Based on subjects ranging from trucks to trees to creepy-crawly insects, these poems are also informative! And because each poem is written for two voices, it requires learners to focus their attention on both reading and listening. As partners take turns reading aloud, they are encouraged to listen to each other in much the same way musicians do as they play a piece of music. Through teamwork and instructive support, students can feel the magic of making a piece of written text come to life.

You'll find that nearly every poem in this collection rhymes. Rhyme and rhythm not only please the ear but also aid comprehension and build vocabulary, both elements of fluency. The poems are also playful. Many contain personification, so that the sun and the moon, and hands and feet—to name a few partners—chat with each other as if they were people. The lessons accompanying each poem are designed to help you use these elements to nurture fluent, expressive readers!

Good poems help us see everyday things in a new way. Poets choose words carefully. They deliver ideas in brief, rhythmic lines. Sound and meaning are equally important. Practicing fluency skills with authentic literary texts can help students develop an appetite for rich literature throughout their reading lives.

So give students the opportunity to experience the joy of poetry while building the skills they need to become fluent and attentive readers, speakers, and listeners. The poems in this collection are here to help you do it—every step of the way!

—*Bobbi Katz*

What Is Fluency?

In his book *The Fluent Reader* (Scholastic, 2003), Timothy Rasinski writes: "Reading fluency refers to the ability of readers to read quickly, effortlessly, and efficiently with good, meaningful expression." As Rasinski and other researchers note, fluency is about much more than merely reading accurately. A fluent reader can recognize words automatically and read them smoothly and rapidly. This ability, known as "automaticity," plays an important role in comprehension (LaBerge and Samuels, 1974 as cited in Blevins, 2001). A certain amount of cognitive energy is involved in reading, whether aloud or to oneself. It makes sense that if students spend less energy on decoding, they have more to spend on comprehension and meaning. And when students are able to focus on comprehension and meaning, they can infuse words and phrases with expression, making sense of the text. Nonfluent reading is often marked by choppiness, as students concentrate on each word rather than the meaning of an entire phrase (Samuels, 1979 as cited in Blevins, 2001). Thus, a student may be able to decode words with accuracy but still not be a fluent reader. In addition to automaticity, reading with fluency involves these essential skills:

Prosody: the ability to read a text orally using appropriate pitch, tone, and rhythm

Phrasing: linking words together into phrases marked by appropriate pauses

Rate: the pace at which one reads

Intonation: the expressive emphasis given to particular words or phrases

Fluent reading does not necessarily come "naturally" along with students' growing ability to accurately decode text. In fact, scientifically based research studies (Chard, Vaughn & Tyler, 2002; Kuhn & Stahl, 2000; National Institute of Child Health and Development, 2000, as cited in Rasinski, 2004) have shown that direct and explicit fluency lessons are an essential part of any literacy program. In its 2000 report, the National Reading Panel indicated that fluency should be a key component of effective instruction.

So how, then, do we teach fluent reading effectively? A number of factors come into play. Of course, it is important to practice repeated readings of texts: The more times students see and hear the text, the more "automatic" it becomes (Samuels, 1979 as cited in Blevins, 2001). Poetry easily lends itself to repeated reading—most poems are relatively short and are meant to be read aloud.

It is essential as well to have students focus on the meaning of text, by asking comprehension questions that keep students actively involved as listeners. And perhaps most important, fluent reading must be modeled. When students are able to see and hear what fluent reading looks and sounds like, they are able to begin mastering the skills themselves. However, modeling fluent reading involves much more than simply reading favorite stories or poems aloud. We must invite students into our heads and help them understand a fluent reader's thought processes. This can be effectively accomplished through think-alouds: taking time during or after oral reading to talk about the reading process itself and offer explicit instruction. Think-alouds may involve pointing out phrasing cues (such as commas) and explaining how they help a reader link words together, calling attention to different kinds of end punctuation and the inflections they require (for more about phrasing cues, see page 10), focusing on literary elements (such as character) and showing students how to bring these elements to life through vocal expression, and so on.

The lessons in this book provide specific strategies to use in your fluency instruction. Poetry that is engaging—along with modeling, whole-group practice, and partnered reading—helps you put students on the road to becoming confident, fluent readers. And with fluency and confidence comes the realization that language can be magical and that reading is fun. Which is, of course, the most important lesson of all.

Meeting the Language Arts Standards

Connections to the McREL Language Arts Standards

The poems and lessons in this book are designed to support you in meeting the following standards for students in grades 2–4, outlined by Mid-continent Research for Education and Learning (McREL), an organization that collects and synthesizes national and state K–12 curriculum standards.

Uses the general skills and strategies of the reading process:

◯ Uses self-correction strategies (for example, searches for cues, identifies miscues, rereads, asks for help)

◯ Reads aloud familiar stories, poems, and passages with fluency and expression (for example, rhythm, flow, meter, tempo, pitch, tone, intonation)

◯ Understands the author's purpose or point of view

◯ Adjusts speed of reading to suit purpose and difficulty of the material

◯ Understands level-appropriate reading vocabulary (for example, synonyms, antonyms, multimeaning words)

Source: *Content Knowledge: A Compendium of Standards and Benchmarks for K–12 Education.* 4th edition (Mid-continent Research for Education and Learning, 2004)

Uses reading skills and strategies to understand and interpret a variety of literary texts:

◯ Understands the ways in which language is used in literary texts (for example, personification, alliteration, onomatopoeia, simile, metaphor, imagery, hyperbole, rhythm)

◯ Makes connections between characters or simple events in a literary work and people or events in his or her own life

Uses listening and speaking strategies for different purposes:

◯ Contributes to group discussions

◯ Asks and responds to questions (for example, about the meaning of a story, about the meaning of words or ideas)

◯ Uses different voice level, phrasing, and intonation for different situations (for example, small-group settings, informal discussions, reports to the class)

◯ Recites and responds to familiar stories, poems, and rhymes with patterns (for example, relates information to own life; describes character, setting, plot)

◯ Uses a variety of verbal communication skills (for example, projection, tone, volume, rate, articulation, pace, phrasing)

Connections to the Reading First Program

The poems and lessons in this book are also designed to support you in implementing the following components of the Reading First program, authorized by the U.S. Department of Education's No Child Left Behind Act.

Vocabulary Development
Development of stored information about the meanings and pronunciation of words necessary for communication, including listening vocabulary, speaking vocabulary, reading vocabulary, and writing vocabulary

Reading Fluency, Including Oral Reading Skills
The ability to read text accurately and quickly

Reading Comprehension Strategies
Strategies for understanding, remembering, and communicating with others about what has been read

Source: *Guidance for the Reading First Program.* (U.S. Department of Education Office of Elementary and Secondary Education, 2002)

Lesson Features

The 20 poems in this book are organized by skill level, from easiest to most challenging. You may choose to move through the poems in order, or select poems for small groups of students at different levels. Each of the poems includes an easy-to-follow one-page lesson guide, followed by the poem itself.

Lesson Overview
In each lesson, you will find the following features:

1 Introduction
A synopsis of the poem or brief description of its theme.

2 Vocabulary
A list of challenging vocabulary words from the poem. You may want to preview pronunciation and/or definitions of these words before reading.

3 Building Fluency With the Poem
A step-by-step guide for fluency instruction, including the following three elements:

4 Model and Discuss
Suggested comprehension questions following the first reading of the text, elements to focus on when performing the modeled reading, and a sample think-aloud script for discussing specific fluency strategies.

5 Whole-Group Practice
Suggestions and strategies for reading the poem aloud with the whole class or group, including echo reading and choral reading.

6 Partner Practice
Suggestions for helping students work with partners to read and practice the poem.

7 Extension Activity
A language arts extension relating to the poem and lesson content. These activities include writing poetry and narrative text, speaking and listening ideas, interactive text displays, and so on.

8 Poem
Reproducible poem pages for creating overheads or individual copies. Each poem is organized like a script, with readers and roles clearly labeled.

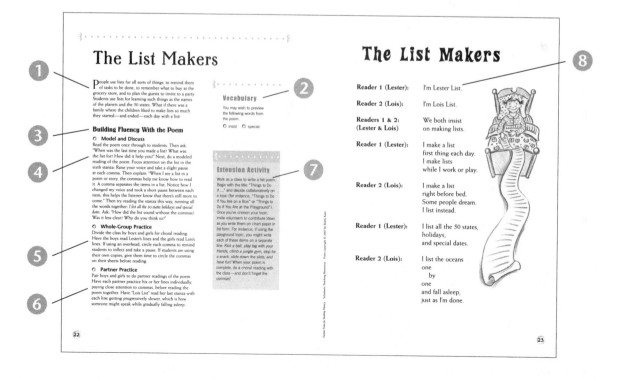

Teaching Tips

Here are some general tips to keep in mind when working with the poems and lessons.

Using an Overhead

You can use the poem pages with an overhead projector for both modeled and whole-group readings. Just copy the sheets onto transparency film and place them on the bed of your projector. This way, all students will be able to see the text as you discuss fluency strategies and perform the choral and echo readings suggested for Whole-Group Practice.

Using Student Copies

If you like, let students use individual copies for reference as you model, discuss, and practice each poem with the group: Simply copy a class set of the reproducible poem pages. In addition, be sure each student has an individual copy of the poem to use during Partner Practice.

Marking the Text

In several lessons, you'll find tips for marking up the poem text (such as highlighting or circling stressed words and punctuation marks). You may also wish to choose your own text elements to mark, according to the individual needs of your class. You can mark the text on an overhead transparency, or guide students in marking up their own copies. (See Practice With Phrase-Cued Text, page 10, for more.)

Making Tape-Recordings

Once partners have mastered a poem, they may wish to record it and add the tape to your listening center for others to enjoy. You might also record poems yourself—students can read along with your recording as they practice the poem with a partner.

Performing the Poems

After completing the Partner Practice section of the lesson, you can have pairs perform the poem for the class. Once students have mastered several poems, you might even organize a show for families, friends, or other classrooms. Have pairs read aloud selections in a Readers Theater performance. If they wish, students can even create costumes and props for their show!

Practice With Phrase-Cued Text

When students read on a slow, word-by-word basis, it is difficult for them to process and comprehend text. Understanding how to put words together in meaningful phrases or chunks and learning how to recognize natural phrase boundaries is an important aid to fluency and comprehension. Research shows that phrase-cued text is an effective tool for helping students to read with appropriate phrasing and intonation (Rasinski, 1990 as cited in Rasinski, 2003).

To create a piece of phrase-cued text, simply highlight a poem or short passage with slashes to indicate natural pauses. One slash (/) indicates a phrase break within a sentence (in poetry, the slash will usually, but not always, occur at the end of a line break); two slashes (//) draw attention to the longer pause at the end of a sentence. See the example, at right, using the poem "Bug Banter" (page 52).

Model good oral reading of the poem or passage, and then invite students to practice using the marked text as a guide for rhythm. After repeated readings, let students read an unmarked copy of the same text to help them apply what they have learned about phrasing.

Bug Banter

Reader 1:
(First Child)
Insects,/ yuk! //
They creep.// They crawl.//
I'd like/ to zap them /
one/ and all.//

Reader 2:
(Second Child)
Yes,/ and boy/ can those guys bite.//
Mosquitoes/ buzzed me/ all last night.//

Reader 1:
(First Child)
They've eaten/ my tomato plants.//

Reader 2:
(Second Child)
What wrecked/ our picnic?//
Flies and ants!//

Reader 1:
(First Child)
Some bugs/ such as ticks/ and fleas/
are expert spreaders/ of disease.//

Readers 1 & 2:
(Both Children)
The insect is/ a useless pest.//
All that it does/ is infest!//

Readers 1 & 2:
(Both Bugs)
Though some consider/ us a curse,/
we're masters/ of the universe!//
There are more insects/ on this planet/
than all/ the animals/ that man it.//
Among/ the many things/ we do,/
we serve as/ Nature's/ Cleanup Crew!//
If left alone/ what we erase/
would make the world/ a rotten place.//
Thanks to us/ the world is sweet./
We chew,/ chew,/ chew/
and eat,/ eat,/ eat.//

Reader 1:
(Bee)
Bees and butterflies—/what power!//
We pollinate/ each tree and flower.//

Reader 2:
(Fruit Fly)
Fruit flies/ must/ top all the lists/
of insects/ who help scientists.//
The speed/ with which/ we multiply/
is something/ on which/ they rely.//

Readers 1 & 2:
(Both Bugs)
On summer nights/ bugs sing and play/
beneath the stars/ until it's day.//

Assessing Fluency

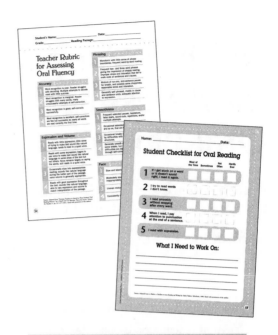

To monitor students' reading informally, ask them to read aloud and listen to how well they attend to key elements of fluency: phrasing (including intonation, stress, and pauses), volume, expression, smoothness, attention to syntax, accuracy, and pace. Use the Teacher Rubric for Assessing Oral Fluency (adapted from Zutell and Rasinski, 1991) on page 12 to track their progress. This assessment allows you to focus on specific aspects of fluency and to note areas in which students have strengths or are in need of further instruction and practice. (When using this rubric, it is helpful to listen to students do a reading several times and evaluate each element separately.) On the scale, scores range between 5 and 20. A student who scores 10 or above is progressing well; scores below 10 signal that a student's reading fluency needs to improve.

Reading specialist Marcia Delany recommends involving students in this process as well. In her book, *Fluency Strategies for Struggling Readers*, she writes, "The more you use the language of fluency, the more focus and attention you draw to the specific expectations you have of your readers and the more consciously and effectively they can work on skills in those areas." Provide students with copies of the Student Checklist for Oral Reading on page 13, model for them how to use it, and then encourage them to monitor their own reading patterns and progress. At the bottom of the checklist, have students record by number the areas in which they need to improve. (Students might also team up with partners and use the checklist to assess each other's reading.)

For more on assessing fluency, consult these sources:

Assessing Reading Fluency by Timothy V. Rasinski (Pacific Resources for Education and Learning, May 2004

Building Fluency: Lessons and Strategies for Reading Success by Wiley Blevins (Scholastic, 2001)

Fluency Strategies for Struggling Readers by Marcia Delany (Scholastic, 2006)

The Fluent Reader by Timothy V. Rasinski (Scholastic, 2003)

3-Minute Reading Assessments: Word Recognition, Fluency, and Comprehension, Grades 1–4 by Timothy V. Rasinski (Scholastic, 2005)

Student's Name:_____ Date:_____

Grade:_____ Reading Passage:_____

Teacher Rubric for Assessing Oral Fluency

In each category, circle the number that best describes the student's performance.

Accuracy

4 Word recognition is excellent; self-corrections are few but successful.

3 Word recognition is good; self-corrects successfully.

2 Word recognition is marginal. Reader struggles with many words; many unsuccessful attempts at self-correction.

1 Word recognition is poor. Reader struggles with decoding. Multiple attempts to decode meet with little success.

Expression and Volume

4 Reads with good expression; sounds like natural language; varies expression and volume to match interpretation of the passage.

3 Occasionally slips into flat reading; sounds like natural language most of the time; voice volume is generally appropriate.

2 Reads with some expression; begins to make text sound like natural language sometimes; focus remains largely on saying the words; reads in a quiet voice.

1 Reads with little expression; little sense of trying to make text sound like natural language; tends to read in a quiet voice.

Phrasing

4 Generally well phrased, mostly in clause and sentence units.

3 Mixture of run-ons, mid-sentence pauses for breath, and possibly some choppiness; reasonable stress and intonation.

2 Frequent choppy reading; improper stress and intonation that fail to mark ends of sentences and clauses.

1 Monotonic with little sense of phrase boundaries; frequent word-by-word reading.

Smoothness

4 Generally smooth reading with some breaks; word and structure difficulties are resolved quickly; usually self-corrects.

3 Occasional breaks in smoothness caused by difficulties with specific words and/or structures.

2 Occasional extended pauses, hesitations, and so on, that are frequent and disruptive.

1 Frequent extended pauses, hesitations, sound-outs, repetitions, or multiple attempts.

Pace

4 Consistently conversational and appropriate.

3 Uneven mixture of fast and slow reading.

2 Moderately slow (or overly and inappropriately fast).

1 Slow and laborious.

Source: Adapted from "Training Teachers to Attend to Their Students' Oral Reading Fluency," by J. Zutell and T.V. Rasinski, *Theory Into Practice*, Volume 30, Number 3, pp. 211-217 (1991). Used with permission of the authors.

Name: _____ **Date:** _____

Student Checklist for Oral Reading

	Most of the Time	Sometimes	Not Often	Hardly Ever
1 If I get stuck on a word or it doesn't sound right, I read it again.	☐	☐	☐	☐
2 I try to read words I don't know.	☐	☐	☐	☐
3 I read smoothly without stopping after every word.	☐	☐	☐	☐
4 When I read, I pay attention to punctuation at the end of a sentence.	☐	☐	☐	☐
5 I read with expression.	☐	☐	☐	☐

What I Need to Work On:

_____

_____

_____

_____

Source: Adapted from *35 Rubrics & Checklists to Assess Reading and Writing* by Adele Fiderer. Scholastic, 1998. Used with permission of the author.

On the Go!

Children always seem to be on the go—running after a Frisbee, catching a softball, playing tag, skipping rope. The wonderful thing about keeping active is that it's not only lots of fun, it's also terrific exercise! This simple poem celebrates children's natural energy as well as the benefits it brings.

Building Fluency With the Poem

Model and Discuss

After reading the poem aloud once through, help children connect to personal experience by asking: "What are some of your favorite sports or activities? How do you feel after running and playing? How do these things help keep you healthy?" Next, do a modeled reading of the poem, focusing on phrasing and rate. Take quick pauses at line breaks, and longer pauses at punctuation marks (periods and commas). Introduce children to the importance of phrasing and rate with a think-aloud: "When a sentence is short and simple, such as *I like to skate*, I group all the words together and say them quickly, one right after another. For a longer sentence, it helps to break up the words. Notice how I read *A good long run (pause) makes me feel great*. This helps the listener keep track of the ideas and gives the language a rhythm."

Whole-Group Practice

Do a line-by-line echo reading of the poem, having students repeat after you. Encourage them to match your speed, phrasing, and intonation.

Partner Practice

Divide the class into pairs, assigning each partner a role (Reader 1 and Reader 2). Remind them to group words in short sentences or phrases together, taking a pause between. Also encourage children to think about the poem's meaning as they read: It's all about action, so invite them to give their voices energy and enthusiasm! After one or two readings, partners can switch roles.

Vocabulary

You may wish to preview the following words from the poem:

- hike
- ski

Extension Activity

Invite children to create their own rhyming poems about a favorite sport or activity. They can begin by writing the activity word on scrap paper and then brainstorming a list of other words that rhyme. For instance, a student who likes to play ball might come up with *tall, all, small, fall,* and so on. Next, have students use their word lists to create a rhyme, such as *I like to play basketball. The net is high and I am small. But I'll reach better when I'm tall!*

On the Go!

Reader 1:   I like to ski.

Reader 2:   I like to skate.

Reader 1:   A good long run
makes me feel great.

Reader 2:   I like to hike.

Reader 1:   I like to bike.

Reader 2:   A nice cool swim
is what I like.

Readers 1 & 2:   All these things are fun to do.
And what's more,
they're good for you!

Partner Poems for Building Fluency Scholastic Teaching Resources Poem copyright © 2007 by Bobbi Katz.

Trailer Truck

From food to furniture, from computers to bicycles, 18-wheelers travel across the country to deliver the goods! Children may not realize that a trailer truck has two parts: a compact cab with an engine that powers the cab itself, under the control of a driver, and a trailer, which carries the heavy load. The trailer cannot move when it is detached from the cab.

Building Fluency With the Poem

Model and Discuss

Before reading, name the two parts of the truck and explain to students what each one does. Then read the poem aloud and ask: "How does the cab help the trailer travel? What's the trailer's job? How do they work together?" Next, do a modeled reading of the poem, paying special attention to end punctuation. Raise your voice at question marks to show the inflection, and use a happy, excited tone for exclamations. Explain: "When I see a question mark at the end of a sentence, I change my voice to show that someone is asking something. An exclamation point can mean someone is happy, excited, or angry. In this poem, I can tell that the exclamation points show happiness and excitement. I use my voice to express those feelings, which helps the listener feel them, too!"

Whole-Group Practice

If using an overhead, use one color highlighter to mark question marks and another to highlight exclamation points. If students are reading from their own copies, provide them with highlighters and have them mark up the page themselves. Then do a choral reading of the poem, encouraging students to follow your inflections for exclamations and questions.

Partner Practice

Let students take turns playing cab and trailer as they read the poem with partners. Encourage them to listen closely to each other and create a rhythm with their voices, especially in the last stanza: Just like the cab and trailer, students must work together!

Vocabulary

You may wish to preview the following words from the poem:

- freight
- whiz
- interstate

Extension Activity

Invite students to name other things that make good partners, such as peanut butter and jelly, spaghetti and meatballs, or pencil and paper. Encourage each student to pick one set of "perfect partners" to write about in a short paragraph. To spark ideas, ask questions such as "What does each partner do by itself? How do these two items work together? What makes the partnership special?" Invite students to share their "partner paragraphs" aloud with the group.

Trailer Truck

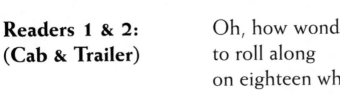

Readers 1 & 2:
(Cab & Trailer)

We are buddies.
What a pair!
We go together
everywhere.

Reader 1 (Cab):

What's a cab
without a trailer?

Reader 2 (Trailer):

Like a ship
without a sailor!

Reader 1 (Cab):

We whiz along the interstate.

Reader 2 (Trailer):

From coast to coast we carry freight.

Readers 1 & 2:
(Cab & Trailer)

Oh, how wonderful it feels
to roll along
on eighteen wheels!

Partner Poems for Building Fluency   Scholastic Teaching Resources   Poem copyright © 1997 by Bobbi Katz.

River Pals

Some jobs work best with teamwork—and a tugboat and barge make a great team! A tugboat may seem tiny compared to a giant barge loaded with goods, but its role is instrumental in getting those goods across the river. With this playful poem, students see that pals come in all shapes and sizes—and even the littlest friend can be a great big help!

Building Fluency With the Poem

↻ Model and Discuss

Before reading, explain to students that tugboats and barges work together to take supplies up and down rivers. The little tugboat pulls the heavy barge along. (Compare to "Trailer Truck," page 17, if you wish.) Then read the poem aloud and ask: "What does this poem tell you about partnership and friendship? How do the tugboat and barge work together?" Next, do a modeled reading of the poem, taking a pause after each period. Explain: "A period tells me that I've come to the end of the sentence, and that means the thought is complete. I take a pause after a period to show that one idea has ended and another is about to begin. In this poem, the pauses also tell the listener when the speaker is changing."

↻ Whole-Group Practice

Divide the class into two groups for a choral reading. Have one group read the tugboat's lines and the other read the barge's lines. The whole class can join together for the last two lines. Encourage groups to listen carefully to one another; when one group completes a line, the other group should wait a beat before chiming in.

↻ Partner Practice

Divide the class into pairs, assigning one partner to play the tugboat and the other to play the barge. Before reading, students might like to highlight each period on the poem sheet; this will help them with phrasing, reminding them to pause before changing speakers. After a few readings, students can switch roles.

Vocabulary

You may wish to preview the following words from the poem:

↻ barge   ↻ lug

↻ haul   ↻ tugboat

Extension Activity

Invite students to think of a time when a friend helped them to get a big job done. It could be anything from hanging a poster in a room to studying for a spelling test. How did the friend help? Did working together make the job easier? Encourage students to write a short paragraph about the experience and draw a picture. They can then present the finished piece to their helping "pal" as a thank-you!

River Pals

Reader 1 (Tugboat):   I'm a tugboat.

Reader 2 (Barge):   I'm a barge.

Reader 1 (Tugboat):   I'm short and fat.

Reader 2 (Barge):   I'm long and large.

Reader 1 (Tugboat):   I can push and I can tug.

Reader 2 (Barge):   I've got a lot of stuff to lug.

Reader 1 (Tugboat):   When you have something to deliver,
I will haul you up the river!

Readers 1 & 2:
(Tugboat & Barge)   Don't we make a perfect pair?
We go together everywhere!

Partner Poems for Building Fluency   Scholastic Teaching Resources   Poem copyright © 2007 by Bobbi Katz.

Numbers and Letters

Numbers tell us what time it is, how much something costs, and which house on a street is the one we want to find. People use letters to form words to communicate ideas, tell stories, and of course, create poetry! In this poem, a number and a letter speak up as if they were people to tell us some of the things they can do.

Building Fluency With the Poem

Model and Discuss

Read the poem to students, and ask: "When was the last time a number helped you? In what ways have you used numbers today? How about letters?" Next, do a modeled reading of the poem, focusing on its rhythm. You can do this by using your voice to emphasize stressed syllables: "I'm a num-ber/ I'm a let-ter/ I'm a count-er/ I spell bet-ter." After reading, explain: "Many poems have a musical quality: a special rhythm, or beat. This makes them fun to read, and fun to listen to! I raised my voice on accented syllables to help the listener hear and feel the beat."

Whole-Group Practice

Divide the class into two groups—numbers and letters. Have each group read its lines chorally. To emphasize rhythm, have one group clap out the beat as the other group reads its part. Then have groups switch roles and repeat.

Partner Practice

Before reading, have partners decide on roles. Encourage each student to look at his or her lines and use a pencil to underline the syllables he or she thinks should be stressed for rhythm. After reading the poem aloud, partners can critique each other—do they think their partner stressed the right syllables? If not, they can erase their previous markings and try again.

Vocabulary

You may wish to preview the following words from the poem:

○ feathery   ○ report

○ maple

Extension Activity

Invite children to use letters to write a poem about numbers! Have each student pick a number and write a poem or paragraph about it. (Poems can be free verse; they don't need to rhyme.) The number could speak as if it were a person! To spark ideas, you can give students these prompts: *My favorite number is _____; It tells me _____; When I see my number, it makes me think of _____.* For instance, a student whose favorite number is two might write: *It tells me how many hands I have; It makes me think of friendship; It is the perfect number of people for playing a game of catch.*

Numbers and Letters

Reader 1 (Number):   I'm a number.

Reader 2 (Letter):   I'm a letter.

Reader 1 (Number):   I'm a counter.

Reader 2 (Letter):   I spell better.

Reader 1 (Number):   I can add
and I subtract.
That's the way
that numbers act!

Reader 2 (Letter):   I form words
both long and short
that tell a story
I report!

Reader 1 (Number):   I count four sparrows
in a tree.
One flies away.
Now there are three!

Reader 2 (Letter):   Three sparrows
small and feathery
sing birdsongs
in a maple tree.
I'll turn them into poetry!

The List Makers

People use lists for all sorts of things: to remind them of tasks to be done, to remember what to buy at the grocery store, and to plan the guests to invite to a party. Students use lists for learning such things as the names of the planets and the 50 states. What if there was a family where the children liked to make lists so much they started—and ended—each day with a list!

Building Fluency With the Poem

◌ Model and Discuss

Read the poem once through to students. Then ask: "When was the last time you made a list? What was the list for? How did it help you?" Next, do a modeled reading of the poem. Focus attention on the list in the sixth stanza: Raise your voice and take a slight pause at each comma. Then explain: "When I see a list in a poem or story, the commas help me know how to read it. A comma separates the items in a list. Notice how I changed my voice and took a short pause between each item; this helps the listener know that there's still more to come." Then try reading the stanza this way, running all the words together: *I list all the 50 states holidays and special dates.* Ask: "How did the list sound without the commas? Was it less clear? Why do you think so?"

◌ Whole-Group Practice

Divide the class by boys and girls for choral reading. Have the boys read Lester's lines and the girls read Lois's lines. If using an overhead, circle each comma to remind students to inflect and take a pause. If students are using their own copies, give them time to circle the commas on their sheets before reading.

◌ Partner Practice

Pair boys and girls to do partner readings of the poem. Have each partner practice his or her lines individually, paying close attention to commas, before reading the poem together. Have "Lois List" read her last stanza with each line getting progressively slower, which is how someone might speak while gradually falling asleep.

Vocabulary

You may wish to preview the following words from the poem:

◌ insist   ◌ special

Extension Activity

Work as a class to write a list poem. Begin with the title "Things to Do If…," and decide collaboratively on a topic (for instance, "Things to Do If You Are on a Bus" or "Things to Do If You Are at the Playground"). Once you've chosen your topic, invite volunteers to contribute ideas as you write them on chart paper in list form. For instance, if using the playground topic, you might write each of these items on a separate line: *Kick a ball, play tag with your friends, climb a jungle gym, stop for a snack, slide down the slide, and have fun!* When your poem is complete, do a choral reading with the class—and don't forget the commas!

The List Makers

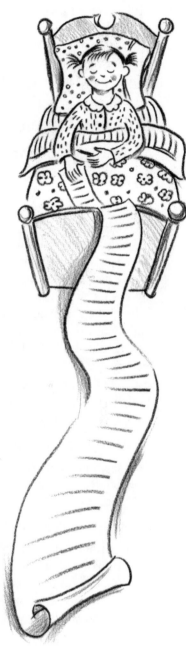

Reader 1 (Lester): I'm Lester List.

Reader 2 (Lois): I'm Lois List.

Readers 1 & 2:
(Lester & Lois)

We both insist
on making lists.

Reader 1 (Lester):

I make a list
first thing each day.
I make lists
while I work or play.

Reader 2 (Lois):

I make a list
right before bed.
Some people dream.
I list instead.

Reader 1 (Lester):

I list all the 50 states,
holidays,
and special dates.

Reader 2 (Lois):

I list the oceans
one
        by
one
and fall asleep,
just as I'm done.

Tree Talk

Trees come in all shapes and sizes; they often change with the seasons. Trees are home to many birds and other animals, and, of course, some trees are great for climbing! Explore the wonderful world of trees with a palm, a pine, and a wise old oak as your guides.

Building Fluency With the Poem

☉ Model and Discuss

Read the poem aloud once through, and ask: "How are palm trees and pine trees alike?" (*Both are somewhat arrogant. Each one thinks its way of being a tree is the only way!*) "How are they different? Is either of these trees good for climbing?" Then do a modeled reading of the poem, emphasizing questions, exclamations, and dialogue. Have students focus on these elements with a think-aloud: "Notice how my voice changes as I read the pine tree's question. When I see a question mark, I know to raise my voice slightly at the end of the sentence. When I read the line *But what a stalk!* the exclamation point tells me to make my voice sound excited. The quotation marks in the last stanza tell me a third character is speaking. I use a different voice for dialogue so the listener can keep track of who is talking."

☉ Whole-Group Practice

Do an echo reading of the poem, pausing every two lines to let students repeat after you. Stress punctuation and dialogue, encouraging students to match your inflections.

☉ Partner Practice

Have partners take turns playing the palm and the pine, thinking about how the characters might speak. Encourage them to speak in unison as the oak tree, paying attention to rhythm, phrasing, and the punctuation cues they practiced in the group lesson.

Vocabulary

You may wish to preview the following words from the poem:

☉ diversity   ☉ stalk

☉ fronds

Extension Activity

Take children on a walk around the school neighborhood and let each student choose a favorite tree. It might be a maple on the playground or an evergreen near the entrance to school. Back in the classroom, invite students to let their tree "talk" by writing a paragraph from the tree's point of view! To spark ideas, ask questions such as: "What does your tree see each day? Does your tree change throughout the year? How does this make it feel?" Let students share their "tree autobiographies" aloud with the class.

Tree Talk

Reader 1 (Palm):   It seems
very strange to me
that people say
you are a tree.

Reader 2 (Pine):   Who, pray tell,
are you to talk?
All you are
is a single stalk.

Reader 1 (Palm):   But what a stalk!
So straight and tall
with fronds like fans
that top it all.

Reader 2 (Pine):   Your trunk is tall.
I must agree.
But look at the branches
that cover me.

**Readers 1 & 2:
(Oak)**   "Listen," said
the old oak tree.
"Our planet needs diversity:
apple, plum, pear, peach,
chestnut, walnut, birch, beech…
Mother Nature thinks it's fine:
Some trees are palm
and some are pine."

Partner Poems for Building Fluency   Scholastic Teaching Resources   Poem copyright © 2007 by Bobbi Katz.

Conversation With a Kite

Kite flying is an age-old pastime, beloved by generations of children and adults. This poem's lovely imagery, imaginative dialogue, and lilting rhythm capture the wonder and joy.

Building Fluency With the Poem

○ Model and Discuss

After reading the poem once through, help children relate to personal experience by asking: "Have you ever flown a kite or seen one flying in the sky? How did it make you feel? How do you think the child in this poem feels about the kite?" Then do a modeled reading of the poem, taking pauses at commas as you point them out in the text. Explain to students: "When we speak, we group certain words together and then take a breath before we continue. The same is true for reading—a comma tells you when to take a breath." Then read the first line of the poem two ways: once without stopping, and once taking pauses at the commas. Ask: "Which way sounds better? Why?"

○ Whole-Group Practice

Do a line-by-line echo reading of the poem, having students repeat after you and match your rhythm. Then divide the class into two groups: children and kites. Have each group read its lines chorally. To emphasize commas and the pauses they indicate, try giving a clap at each one.

○ Partner Practice

Have partners take on roles and practice their parts individually before coming together. Have students read aloud to themselves softly, reminding them to pay special attention to commas and phrasing. When each reader is ready, partners can read the whole poem as a conversation. Then have children switch roles and repeat the exercise.

Vocabulary

You may wish to preview the following words from the poem:

○ gliding ○ whirl-away

○ runaway

Extension Activity

Encourage students to name favorite playthings, such as a stuffed animal, a jump rope, or even a soccer ball. If they could have a conversation with this item, what would they say to it? What might the toy say back? Pair students up to invent their own dialogue: One student plays the child and the other plays the toy. Children can conduct "interviews," for instance: (Child) "How do you feel when you get tossed across the field?" (Baseball) "I love flying through the air as fast as I can!" You might have children tape-record their dialogues; then place the tapes in the listening center for other students to enjoy.

Conversation With a Kite

Reader 1:
(Child)
Come back, come back, my runaway kite!
Come back and play with me!

Reader 2:
(Kite)
I'm riding and gliding on whirl-away winds.
I'm going somewhere. Can't you see?

Reader 1:
(Child)
Where are you going my beautiful kite,
flying so high in the sky?

Reader 2:
(Kite)
I'm going to visit the lost balloons.
I must fly away, fly away, fly!

Reader 1:
(Child)
When I hold your string, oh my magical kite,
why do I feel the wind in my hand?

Reader 2:
(Kite)
The wind is a taste of the sky, my young friend,
that I give to a child of the land.

Partner Poems for Building Fluency Scholastic Teaching Resources Poem copyright © 1989 by Random House. Used with permission of Bobbi Katz.

Musically Speaking

Poetry has a lot in common with music. In fact, the words to songs are called lyrics and most rhyming poetry is called lyrical. Like music, poems can have different rhythms and can tell stories. This poem provides information about music as it experiments with the rhythm, tone, and musicality of spoken language.

Building Fluency With the Poem

○ Model and Discuss

After reading the poem aloud, check comprehension by asking: "How many singers sing a solo? A duet? A trio? A quartet?" You can also bring in personal experience by having students name their favorite musical recordings, telling why they like them and how many singers and instruments perform them. Next, do a modeled reading of the poem. Call attention to the rhythm and musical qualities by emphasizing line breaks and stressing rhyming words. Explain: "Many poems can sound like music when we read them aloud. Notice how I paused slightly after each line and raised my voice on the rhyming words. This helps emphasize the poem's rhythm, making it sound almost like a song."

○ Whole-Group Practice

Try the "phrase-cued text" technique using an overhead. Draw one slash after each line break, and two slashes after end punctuation marks. (If students are reading from individual copies, help them mark up their own pages.) Explain that one slash indicates a short pause and two indicate a longer one. Do a choral reading of the poem, using the phrasing cues as a guide for rhythm. (See Practice With Phrase-Cued Text, page 10, for more.)

○ Partner Practice

In addition to phrase-cue slashes, partners might benefit from underlining the rhyming words on their sheets (*song/along, solo/polo*, and so on). Have pairs of students take turns reading their lines, stressing rhymes to emphasize the beat.

Vocabulary

You may wish to preview the following words from the poem:

- ○ duet ○ solo
- ○ polo ○ trio
- ○ quartet

Extension Activity

Help students think about the tonal qualities of music by connecting it to moods. On chart paper, create columns for different emotions: "Happy Music," "Sad Music," "Exciting Music," and so on. Then have volunteers suggest songs for each section. As a class, discuss why and how each evokes the mood. For a further extension, invite students to each choose a favorite song and write a paragraph explaining how it makes them feel and why.

Musically Speaking

Reader 1: A single person
who sings a song
with no one else
to sing along
is singing a solo.
(And *not* playing polo.)

Reader 2: There hasn't been a duet yet
with less than two musicians.
And they may sing
or play a tune
in various positions.

Reader 1: It takes three-o
to make a trio.

Reader 2: But take four
and I bet
that you'll get
a quartet.

Readers 1 & 2: Lots of singers?
Don't ignore us!
We're the gang
that's called the chorus.
With instruments?
Then what you see
is a marching band
or a symphony.

Partner Poems for Building Fluency   Scholastic Teaching Resources   Poem copyright © 2007 by Bobbi Katz.

Sun and Moon

The sun and moon have inspired countless poems, myths, legends, and stories throughout history. Weaving scientific fact with poetic, lyrical language, this piece invites students to compare and contrast two major features of the sky.

Building Fluency With the Poem

Model and Discuss

Read the poem aloud, and ask: "How are the sun and moon alike and different? What kinds of activities do you like to do on a sunny day? How about on a moonlit night?" Do a modeled reading of the poem, focusing on vocal expression. Reading expressively is an extremely important part of fluency; demonstrate by giving your voice a bright, bouncy tone for the lines of the Sun and a soothing, mysterious quality for the Moon. Then ask: "In my reading, did you notice a difference between the Sun's verses and the Moon's verses? How did my voice change? This poem uses descriptive language to contrast two different things. I used my voice to help the listener feel the difference between a bright, sunny day and a dark, moonlit night."

Whole-Group Practice

Go through the poem verse by verse, inviting several volunteers to try their own vocal interpretations for each stanza. Encourage partners to think about how the sun and moon make them feel and to use their voices to express that feeling as they read. As a group, discuss similarities and differences among children's readings.

Partner Practice

The poem is an imaginary conversation between the sun and moon. In what tones of voice might they speak to each other? Encourage students to try out different moods and emotions. Then have them switch roles.

Vocabulary

You may wish to preview the following words from the poem:

- charm
- reflect
- distant
- satellite

Extension Activity

Invite students to express the special qualities of the sun or moon by writing an acrostic poem. Have them write the letters *S-U-N* or *M-O-O-N* down the left side of a sheet of paper and then write a descriptive word or phrase beginning with each letter. For example: *Starts the day; Ultra-hot; Nature's energy.* Or: *Mysterious; Overhead; Orbiting around us; Nighttime friend.* If children are stumped for words, let them look through a picture dictionary for ideas. When the poems are complete, let students share their work with the group.

Sun and Moon

Reader 1 (Sun):

I'm the Sun.
I make the day.
Earth turns toward me.
Night fades away.

Reader 2 (Moon):

I'm the Moon,
and since my birth
each month I loop
around the Earth.

Reader 1 (Sun):

I'm quite different
than you are.
I'm heat and light.
I am a star.

Reader 2 (Moon):

Dark and cold,
I'm only bright
when I reflect
your distant light.
What is the Moon?
Earth's satellite.

Reader 1 (Sun):

I light the day.

Reader 2 (Moon):

I charm the night.

Partner Poems for Building Fluency   Scholastic Teaching Resources   Poem copyright © 2007 by Bobbi Katz.

The Punctuators

Staying aware of end punctuation is an important part of reading, whether one is reading alone or for an audience. This poem introduces the period, the question mark, and the exclamation point, allowing students to review punctuation and practice fluency at the same time!

Building Fluency With the Poem

Model and Discuss

Read the poem and review the concepts by asking: "When do you use a period? What kind of sentence do you end with a question mark? When should you use an exclamation point?" Next, do a modeled reading of the poem. Exaggerate your inflections to indicate end punctuation: Use a declarative tone for periods, raise your voice at the ends of questions, and place extra stress on exclamations. Use your voice differently to read the bolded titles within the poem, pausing before moving on to the text below. Explain: "When I see headings, or titles, in a text, I know they're separate from the rest of the reading. I pause between the title and the text that follows. This poem is all about punctuation, so I paid extra-special attention to the periods, question marks, and exclamation points. How did my voice change for each one?"

Whole-Group Practice

Do a whole-group echo reading of the poem, stanza by stanza. Encourage students to imitate your inflections as closely as possible. If you like, you can use a different color highlighter to highlight each punctuation mark on an overhead, or have students highlight the punctuation on their own copies.

Partner Practice

Have pairs read the poem, encouraging them to pay particular attention to the titles and punctuation marks. Then have students switch roles so that each gets a chance to read each part.

Vocabulary

You may wish to preview the following words from the poem:

- emphatic
- sparingly
- sensation

Extension Activity

Provide students with sentence strips for a "mystery punctuation" game. Have each student write three sentences—one statement, one question, and one exclamation. The trick is, they must leave out the end punctuation mark! When students are finished, place all the strips on a bulletin board. Invite volunteers to choose a sentence, decide what the end punctuation mark should be, and write it on the strip. For instance, *Today is Monday* would take a period; *What time is it* would take a question mark; and *Boy, I'm hungry* would take an exclamation point.

The Punctuators

Readers 1 & 2: At the end of a sentence,
what do you see?
It has to be one
of the following three.

Reader 1: **The Period**
The period is just a dot,
but it gets to do a lot.
A period goes at the end
each time you make a statement,
   friend.

Reader 2: **The Question Mark**
When does a question mark appear?
When do you ask a question, dear?
What do question marks all show?
There's something someone wants to know.

Readers 1 & 2: **The Exclamation Point**
Use sparingly to be dramatic.
Let's go, grammar!
Be emphatic!
Pitch that ball!
Batter, bat it!
Hey, that play's a real sensation!
It deserves an exclamation!

Partner Poems for Building Fluency   Scholastic Teaching Resources   Poem copyright © 1999 by Bobbi Katz from *25 Great Grammar Poems* by Bobbi Katz.

Spring Conversations

Every season has its special sounds: There's the crunch of leaves in autumn, the whoosh of cold winds in winter, and the splash of diving into a swimming pool in summer. In springtime, the weather gets warm and children go outside to play! Invite students to listen up and experience the sounds of their favorite spring activities.

Building Fluency With the Poem

○ Model and Discuss
After reading the poem once through, ask students: "What are some other games you like to play outdoors when the weather gets warm? What sounds do you hear when you do these activities?" Next, do a modeled reading of the poem, placing particular emphasis on the words in special type. Use your voice to imitate each sound. Then point out these words to students and explain: "When I see words in special type, such as italics, boldface, or capital letters, I know to emphasize these words when I read. In this case, each of these words imitates a sound—that's called onomatopoeia. When I read 'noisy' words such as *thud*, *thump*, and *whack*, I use my voice to imitate those sounds. And special type such as capital letters, for example, means I can make the sounds in an extra-loud voice."

○ Whole-Group Practice
If using an overhead, circle each onomatopoetic word (or have students circle in their own copies). Read the body of the poem chorally several times. Each time you come to a word in special type, call on a different volunteer to read that word. Encourage students to use their own special voices to imitate the sounds.

○ Partner Practice
Have students read the poem several times with a partner, trying out different vocal interpretations for the onomatopoetic words. Be sure students switch roles after a few readings, so that each has a chance to read both parts and make every sound in the poem.

Vocabulary

You may wish to preview the following words from the poem:

○ cascading   ○ ripple

○ echoes

Extension Activity

Work as a class to write your own poem using onomatopoeia. Together, come up with an activity, such as going to the beach, playing a game of soccer, or even eating a meal. Invite students to brainstorm sounds associated with the activity, and use these words to write the poem. For instance, a poem about eating after-school snacks might go something like this: *Crunch! go the potato chips; Slurp! goes the milk shake; Chomp! goes the apple; And I say, Mmm!*

Spring Conversations

Reader 1:   **_"Whisk!"_**
whirls the jump rope,
twirling
around.

Reader 2:   **"THUD!"**
say the sneakers,
bouncing off the ground.

Reader 1:   **_"Thumpity, thump, thump!"_**
echoes the concrete
as the basketball
travels
down
the court
across the street.

Reader 2:   **"SMACK!"**
says the ball to the catcher's mitt.

Reader 1:   **"WHACK!"**
says the bat when it makes a hit.

Readers 1 & 2:   The sound of the toss
of a handful of jacks
is a cascading ripple
of **clickety clacks**.

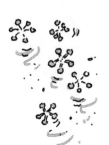

Partner Poems for Building Fluency   Scholastic Teaching Resources   Poem copyright © 2001 by Bobbi Katz from _A Rumpus of Rhymes: A Book of Noisy Poems_ by Bobbi Katz.

Hands and Feet

The human body is an amazing machine. And hands and feet are incredibly useful tools! Hands can button a shirt, tie a shoe, or open a door. Feet can take a stroll, dance a jig, or jump a rope. In this piece, a pair of hands and feet can also "talk"—and tell us about all the wonderful things they can do!

Building Fluency With the Poem

Model and Discuss

After reading the piece aloud, ask: "What activities do your hands help you do? How about your feet?" Next, do a modeled reading of the poem. If using an overhead, sweep your finger under the words as you go, calling attention to the poem's special layout. (If students are following along in their own copies, encourage them to look at the pattern of the words.) As you read, take pauses at line breaks, making each linked phrase "pop" with your voice. Emphasize unusual punctuation (such as an ellipsis in the middle of a phrase) by taking an exaggerated pause. Then explain: "The way words are grouped together in a poem gives us a hint about how it should be read. When line breaks or punctuation separates groups of words, each phrase should be read in a way that makes it stand out. Three dots in a row are called an ellipsis. This means we should take a pause before finishing the sentence."

Whole-Group Practice

Do a choral reading of the poem, emphasizing line breaks and ellipses. To help the group follow your rhythm, you might use conductor-like movements: Hold up a hand to signify "stop," and swing your hand lightly back and forth to say "continue."

Partner Practice

Encourage partners to practice reading one or two stanzas at a time. Explain that in this poem, listening to the other speaker is especially important because the voices respond to each other—at one point, one completes the other's sentence! Once pairs have practiced their timing for small sections, they can read the poem as a whole.

Vocabulary

You may wish to preview the following words from the poem:

- employ
- notion
- locomotion

Extension Activity

Use the poem as a jumping-off point for a discussion about the five senses. Ask: "Which body parts help you to see, hear, smell, touch, and taste?" Have students choose one body part and write a first-person paragraph about it without naming it. Then have students share their "sense riddles" with the class. For instance: *I help you know when your dog is scratching to come inside. The sound of a bell tells me that school is over. I especially like music! What am I?* (ears)

Hands and Feet

Readers 1 & 2:
(Hands & Feet)

We're two pairs
that are hard to beat.

Reader 1 (Hands):

Meet your hands
and…

Reader 2 (Feet):

meet your feet.

Readers 1 & 2:
(Hands & Feet)

We're both couples
in the employ
of almost every girl and boy.
We help you do
what you ask us to.
We take orders
right from you.

Reader 1 (Hands):

A hand has fingers.

Reader 2 (Feet):

A foot has toes.

Readers 1 & 2:
(Hands & Feet)

Five on each
is how that goes.

Reader 1 (Hands):

Fingers are handy
for counting to 10.
For 20 …
and 30
keep counting again.

(continued)

Partner Poems for Building Fluency Scholastic Teaching Resources Poem copyright © 2007 by Bobbi Katz.

Reader 2 (Feet):

The most important
work feet do is…
transportation.

Reader 1 (Hands):

Yes, that's true.

Reader 2 (Feet):

We'll move you
when you get
the notion.
We're your means of
locomotion.
Want to walk

      or

         run

           or skip?
Count on us to make the trip.

Reader 1 (Hands):

A single hand
 can write a book,
  can open a door,
   can unhook a hook.
There's no end to what one hand can do.
Now imagine a pair
working two by two!

Readers 1 & 2:
(Hands & Feet)

We're at your service.
Aren't we neat?

Reader 1 (Hands):

A pair of hands.

Reader 2 (Feet):

A pair of feet.

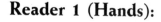

Partner Poems for Building Fluency   Scholastic Teaching Resources

Measure for Measure

Measuring is an essential math skill, both in school and in everyday life. This poem lets students take a whimsical look at the subject of conversation between two important—but very different—measuring tools.

Building Fluency With the Poem

◌ Model and Discuss

After reading the poem aloud, check comprehension by asking: "What does a ruler measure? How about a thermometer? What units of measurement does each one use?" Then do a modeled reading of the poem, emphasizing its conversational tone and question-and-answer format. Raise your voice at the ends of questions, and use an emphatic tone for declarative answers. Explain your reading with a think-aloud: "I see that this poem is a conversation between two characters, a ruler and a thermometer. The characters are just meeting each other, so they have many questions to ask and answer. To help the listener follow the conversation, I raise my voice at the ends of the questions. Then I use a firm voice for the answers."

◌ Whole-Group Practice

Divide the class into two groups, having one group read each role. After practicing the poem several times, bring out the conversational aspect by having each group of students line up in a row, rows facing each other. Encourage each student to speak to the student opposite him or her, having children look up from their papers to make eye contact when possible.

◌ Partner Practice

Divide the class into pairs of thermometers and rulers for partner reading. Encourage students to think of themselves as whichever tool they're playing. Explain that they are meeting each other for the very first time. They might bow or shake hands as they say, "Glad to meet you" and "It's been a pleasure." Have them use their voices to express their curiosity!

Vocabulary

You may wish to preview the following words from the poem:

- ◌ degrees
- ◌ pleasure
- ◌ thermometer

Extension Activity

Invite students to create their own question-and-answer dialogue by conducting personal interviews. (For this activity, you might want to pair students who don't often spend time together.) Have each student write a list of questions for his or her partner, such as "What is your favorite after-school activity? What's your favorite snack? If you could have any animal in the world as a pet, what would you choose?" Remind students that in the poem, the ruler and thermometer discovered that they had many differences but a lot in common, too! After their interviews, encourage partners to discuss how they are alike and different.

Measure for Measure

Reader 1 (Ruler):   I'm a ruler.

Reader 2 (Thermometer):   What's your pleasure?

Reader 1 (Ruler):   As a rule,
I like to measure.

Reader 2 (Thermometer):   Say, I like to measure, too.

Reader 1 (Ruler):   You're not a ruler.
What are you?

Reader 2 (Thermometer):   A thermometer.
I measure heat.

Reader 1 (Ruler):   I measure inches,
       yards,
         and
           feet.

Reader 2 (Thermometer):   That must mean
you measure space.

Reader 1 (Ruler):   Anywhere
     and anyplace.

(continued)

Partner Poems for Building Fluency   Scholastic Teaching Resources   Poem copyright © 2007 by Bobbi Katz.

Reader 2 (Thermometer):   I always measure by degrees.
Will something boil?
Will something freeze?
Is someone sick?
Is someone well?
Check me out and you can tell!

Reader 1 (Ruler):   You mean you
measure cold or hot?

Reader 2 (Thermometer):   That I do and quite a lot.

Reader 1 (Ruler):   Glad to meet you.

Reader 2 (Thermometer):   It's been a pleasure.

Readers 1 & 2:
(Ruler & Thermometer)   We're not the same,
but we both measure.

Bird or Mammal?

Animal classification can sometimes be confusing, but it's an important science skill. In this rhyming conversation, students get a chance to debate the classification rules and to learn a foolproof way to answer the question: Bird or mammal?

Building Fluency With the Poem

○ Model and Discuss

After reading the poem aloud, check comprehension by asking: "What are some characteristics of birds? Of mammals? How can you tell for sure which group an animal belongs to?" Then do a modeled reading of the poem. Slow your rate a bit on the informational passages to help make important scientific facts clear. Also be sure to put extra emphasis on the word *most* in the fourth stanza. Then explain: "This poem has a lot of important information. Notice how I slowed down a bit on lines like *Ostriches weigh much too much/ to fly on muscle power/ but they run faster than birds fly/ at 50 miles an hour!* This is a surprising fact, so I want to make sure the listener can hear and understand it." Next, point out that the word *most* is in italics. "When a word is in italics, that means I should stress it when I read."

Whole-Group Practice

Read the poem chorally several times, leading the group to slow down and enunciate clearly important facts. Guide students to stress specific information, such as the phrases *arctic seas* and *50 miles an hour.*

○ Partner Practice

Before reading, invite partners to use a highlighter to mark the facts they think are most important in the poem. Then have partners take turns reading roles, slowing down and stressing the passages they marked.

Vocabulary

You may wish to preview the following words from the poem:

○ arctic   ○ flightless

○ creature   ○ muscle

Extension Activity

Invite students to sharpen their descriptive language skills with an animal guessing game. Have each student choose a secret animal (bird or mammal) and write a descriptive paragraph about it without naming it. Then have pairs of students trade paragraphs and guess whether the description is about a bird or a mammal. They can then guess the name of the animal. For instance: *This animal wakes farmers up with the sound* cock-a-doodle-do! *It has a red comb on top of its head. It eats corn and grain.* (Bird: rooster)

Bird or Mammal?

Reader 1: Is it a bird or is it a mammal,
such as a dog, a cat, or a camel?

Reader 2: Easy to answer.
Do you know whether
it dresses in fur
or dresses in feather?

Reader 1: All birds fly.
I know that's true.

Reader 2: Buster, I've got news for you.
Most birds fly,
but not all do.

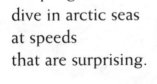

Reader 1: Flightless birds?

Reader 2: There are a few.
Penguins' wings
are useless things
for leaving land and rising,
but penguins
dive in arctic seas
at speeds
that are surprising.

Ostriches weigh much too much
to fly on muscle power,
but they run faster than birds fly
at 50 miles an hour!

Partner Poems for Building Fluency   Scholastic Teaching Resources   Poem copyright © 2007 by Bobbi Katz.

(continued)

Reader 1:   Birds lay eggs!

Reader 2:   Indeed, they do,
                  but certain reptiles
                  lay eggs, too!
                  If it's a bird
                  it has one feature
                  that makes it a bird,
                  not some other creature.

Readers 1 & 2:   We'll know it's a bird
                       when we know whether
                       it dresses in fur
                       or dresses in feather.

Fact and Fiction

Learning the difference between fictional and factual text is an important comprehension skill. In this poem, students read alternating examples of each, which allows them to compare and contrast. Fact and fiction may tell very different stories, and in this case the contrast makes for humorous reading!

Building Fluency With the Poem

○ Model and Discuss

Read the poem aloud to students. Then check comprehension by asking volunteers to name one fact and one piece of fiction from the poem. Next, do a modeled reading of the piece, focusing on vocal expression. Read the "Fact" and "Fiction" labels in a firm, clear voice, taking a pause after the colon. Contrast stanzas by using a more sober voice for facts and a more playful tone for fiction. Then explain: "This poem has a label before each stanza. I read these labels in a clear voice so that listeners know whether the lines that follow will be fact or fiction. Notice that I also read the facts in a different tone of voice from the fiction. Every fact in this poem is true, while the fiction parts are a little outrageous! When I read these parts with different expression, it's another way to help listeners tell the difference between the kinds of text."

○ Whole-Group Practice

Divide the class into two groups, fact and fiction. Guide each group to follow your vocal expression as you read chorally; then have groups switch roles.

○ Partner Practice

After partners have read the poem several times, invite them to have fun with vocal expression by mixing it up! Encourage students to read the fiction stanzas in a serious, newscaster-type tone and the fact stanzas in a storytelling voice. Have students discuss how a change in vocal expression can imply a different meaning.

Vocabulary

You may wish to preview the following words from the poem:

○ astronomers   ○ fiction

○ elliptical   ○ galaxy

○ fact   ○ revolves

Extension Activity

Choose a topic, such as your town or school, and give each student two index cards. Have students write one factual sentence and one fictional sentence about the topic, without indicating the type of sentence. (For instance, fact and fiction sentences about school might read: *Some students ride the bus to school; Everyone flies to school in a helicopter!*) Next, divide a bulletin board in half, labeling one side "Fact" and the other side "Fiction." Place all the cards in a paper bag. Invite students to take turns choosing a card at random, reading the sentence, and placing it on the appropriate part of the board.

Fact and Fiction

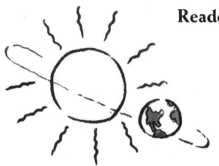

Reader 1:   **Fact:**
The earth revolves
around the sun.
There are eight planets.
Earth is one.

Reader 2:   **Fiction:**
Creatures live
on the planet Mars
with baseball teams
a lot like ours!

Reader 1:   **Fact:**
The Sun is really
another star.
Astronomers study
how many there are.

Reader 2:   **Fiction:**
Every Martian
has seven hands
with seven fingers
like rubber bands.

(continued)

Partner Poems for Building Fluency   Scholastic Teaching Resources   Poem copyright © 2007 by Bobbi Katz.

Reader 1: **Fact:**
The planets revolve
in an elliptical path,
which astronomers plot
by using math.

Reader 2: **Fiction:**
Martians bounce
around the bases
with three blue noses
on their blue faces.

Reader 1: **Fact:**
Telescopes
let people see
way beyond
our galaxy.

Reader 2: **Fiction:**
Martian baseball fans
all like
to see the pitcher
ride a bike.

Readers 1 & 2: Fact always claims that it is true.
Fiction weaves a tale for you.

Two Parts of You

Every person has two special, very different parts: the body and the mind. While they have different jobs, these parts are interconnected. Each sends signals to the other to help keep the whole self functioning well. In this poem, the body and mind speak directly to the reader and tell children how to help them work at their best.

Building Fluency With the Poem

Model and Discuss

Read the poem aloud, and ask: "How does your body help you do things every day? What kinds of jobs does your mind do?" Then do a modeled reading, focusing on punctuation that may be less familiar to students. For instance, pause and inflect at the semicolon in the third stanza; take a longer pause at the colon in the eleventh stanza; and let your voice trail off at the ellipses in the last stanza. As you point out the punctuation marks to students, explain: "A semicolon divides a sentence into two parts. The parts are related, but each contains a different thought. I pause to let the listener know there's more to come. A colon can mean that dialogue is coming. In this case, *Mind* is about to tell us what it is thinking. I take a pause to help the listener follow the idea. Ellipses can break up sentences, too. I take a long pause before completing the sentence. This can make the reading more exciting for listeners—it keeps them guessing how the sentence will end!"

Whole-Group Practice

Do a choral reading of the piece, stopping to focus on special punctuation. Practice the stanzas that include semicolons, colons, and ellipses several times.

Partner Practice

Let partners read the poem together, taking turns with roles. Encourage students to think about the way each character might speak, using their voices to express the conversational tone of the poem as well as focusing on punctuation.

Vocabulary

You may wish to preview the following words from the poem:

- inspired
- realize
- overtired

Extension Activity

Encourage each student to choose a favorite physical activity. Then have children draw a cartoon of themselves doing the activity, including "thought bubbles" for both mind and body. For instance, a child who draws herself playing tag might have her body say, *I'm getting tired.* Meanwhile her mind thinks, *I'm going to stop for a snack. My body needs some rest and energy.* Have students share their cartoons and read the thought bubbles aloud, using a different voice for each.

Two Parts of You

Reader 1 (Body):   I'm your body.

Reader 2 (Mind):   I'm your mind.

Readers 1 & 2:
(Body & Mind)   We're the best friends
you can find.
Both of us like exercise.
But different sorts;
please, realize.

Reader 1 (Body):   I like to run and ride a bike.

Reader 2 (Mind):   Solving stuff is what I like.
I'm the part of you that thinks.

Reader 1 (Body):   I'm the part of you that drinks.

Reader 2 (Mind):   Juice? Milk? Lemonade?
I'm where the decision's made.

Reader 1 (Body):   I take you where you want to go.

Reader 2 (Mind):   What you should do
is what I know.
For example, if it's hot,
a body needs to drink a lot.

Partner Poems for Building Fluency   Scholastic Teaching Resources   Poem copyright © 2007 by Bobbi Katz.

(continued)

Reader 1 (Body):   Mind tells me where
and how to get
drinks to keep
my whistle wet.

Reader 2 (Mind):   I think:
How can a kid get cool?
Jump into a swimming pool!

Readers 1 & 2:   We both do best
(Body & Mind)   If we get rest.

Reader 1 (Body):   I'll win the race.

Reader 2 (Mind):   I'll ace the test.

Readers 1 & 2:   But…
(Body & Mind)   when we get
overtired,
neither of us is
inspired.
So…
listen to our signals, kid.
You'll be happy that you did.

Partner Poems for Building Fluency   Scholastic Teaching Resources

Bug Banter

Creepy, crawly, icky, sticky bugs—they're often called "pests," but these tiny creatures actually help us in lots of ways! Invite students to learn just how important bugs can be.

Building Fluency With the Poem

○ Model and Discuss

Read the poem aloud, and ask: "How did you feel about bugs before hearing this poem? Has your opinion changed? How?" Next, do a modeled reading. Help students recognize the point-of-view change by using two distinct voices: one for the children's lines and another for the insects' lines. In addition, take a deep breath and a long pause between the first and second page, helping to signify the change in narrator. Explain your reading with a think-aloud: "In this poem, there are two kinds of voices—people and bugs—and each has a very different opinion. To help the listener distinguish between the two points of view, I used a special voice for each. I also stopped for a moment when the narrator's voice was about to change. This gives listeners time to think about the ideas in the first part of the poem before I move on to the second part."

○ Whole-Group Practice

Divide the class into two groups—children and bugs—and then divide each group into two mini-groups (First Child, Second Child; Bees, Fruit Flies). Before reading, let each group decide on distinctive voices for their characters. Then practice the poem several times, having each small group read its lines chorally.

○ Partner Practice

Have partners assign themselves roles before reading: One student reads the lines for First Child and Bee, and the partner reads the lines for Second Child and Fruit Fly. All other parts are read in unison. Remind students to use different voices for each of their parts and to pause between the first and second pages of the poem.

Vocabulary

You may wish to preview the following words from the poem:

○ banter   ○ mosquitoes

○ infest   ○ pollinate

Extension Activity

Go outside on an insect walk. Encourage students to point out the bugs they see, taking note of what each insect is doing. Then have students form small groups to write or improvise buggy mini-plays! Have each group focus on a different type of insect, inventing dialogue for the creatures. For instance: (Ant 1) *I need help carrying this sand to our hill!* (Ant 2) *Sure! You carry one grain and I'll carry another.* Let groups perform for the class, keeping the name of their insect a secret. Then have the class guess the bug from the dialogue!

Bug Banter

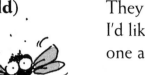

Reader 1:
(First Child)

Insects, yuk!
They creep. They crawl.
I'd like to zap them
one and all.

Reader 2:
(Second Child)

Yes, and boy can those guys bite.
Mosquitoes buzzed me all last night.

Reader 1:
(First Child)

They've eaten my tomato plants.

Reader 2:
(Second Child)

What wrecked our picnic?
Flies and ants!

Reader 1:
(First Child)

Some bugs such as ticks and fleas
are expert spreaders of disease.

Readers 1 & 2:
(Both Children)

The insect is a useless pest.
All that it does is infest!

Partner Poems for Building Fluency   Scholastic Teaching Resources   Poem copyright © 2007 by Bobbi Katz.

Readers 1 & 2:
(Both Bugs)

Though some consider us a curse,
we're masters of the universe!
There are more insects on this planet
than all the animals that man it.
Among the many things we do,
we serve as Nature's Cleanup Crew!
If left alone what we erase
would make the world a rotten place.
Thanks to us the world is sweet.
We chew, chew, chew
and eat, eat, eat.

Reader 1 (Bee):

Bees and butterflies—what power!
We pollinate each tree and flower.

Reader 2:
(Fruit Fly)

Fruit flies must top all the lists
of insects who help scientists.
The speed with which we multiply
is something on which they rely.

Readers 1 & 2:
(Both Bugs)

On summer nights bugs sing and play
beneath the stars until it's day.

The Wind

The wind changes with each season. Winter winds can be fierce, while summer winds are often gentle. In this poem, the wind of each of the four seasons speaks with noisy words as it reveals its character.

Building Fluency With the Poem

Model and Discuss

After reading the poem, ask: "How does the wind change where we live? What is it like in each season?" Then do a modeled reading, focusing on characterization—emphasize words and phrases that tell about each wind's personality. Also stress the words in special type (all capitals, italics). Explain: "In this poem, the language tells a lot about the personality of each season's wind—this is called characterization. The poet uses onomatopoeia—words that sound like their meaning, such as *swoosh*, *crunching*, and *hissss*. When I read a phrase such as *I am the magician. ABRACADABRA!* it tells me that the spring wind is mischievous and makes quick changes. The words in all capitals and italics also give me clues—I know to give extra stress to those words. Notice how the poet also uses a made-up word, *huffle;* context clues help me understand what it means. When you read a story or poem with different characters, look for words that tell you what each character is like. Paying special attention to those words helps listeners get to know the character better.

Whole-Group Practice

Break the class into four groups, one for each season. Before reading, let students meet to discuss their character's traits (playful, gentle, spooky, or fierce). Then come together and have each group read its lines chorally, emphasizing characterization.

Partner Practice

Have pairs of students assign themselves two roles each: Spring/Fall or Summer/Winter. Before reading, students can underline words and phrases that show characterization; have them use their markings to guide their readings.

Vocabulary

You may wish to preview the following words from the poem:

- daffodils   - rustle
- hammock

Extension Activity

Invite students to write four short "character descriptions" of something else that changes with each season, such as trees, activities we do, or even foods we eat. Encourage them to use vivid adjectives—for instance: *The foods of winter warm your chilly bones. Soup and hot cocoa are yummy and piping hot! The foods of spring are crunchy and leafy, like fresh veggies from the garden. The foods of summer are juicy and sweet, like a plum or a peach. The foods of fall are for family—turkey and pumpkin pie for all!* Let students share their seasonal descriptions aloud with the group.

The Wind

Reader 1:

Spring
I am the wind of spring…
Hold tight to your kite
the day I come to play!
Feel me in your hand—
tugging-tugging.
I am the magician.
ABRACADABRA!
See the daffodils bend
and hear them rustle
at my command.

Reader 2:

Summer
I am the wind of summer.
The welcome wind.
Gently swooshing
against your hot cheeks
at the playground
and twirling your pinwheel.
I woof the sailboats across the water
and cool the sweaty players
on the baseball fields.
Doze on a hammock—
I'll be gently swooshing through
your dreams…
Swooosh… Swooosh…

Partner Poems for Building Fluency   Scholastic Teaching Resources   Poem copyright © 2001 by Bobbi Katz from *A Rumpus of Rhymes: A Book of Noisy Poems* by Bobbi Katz.

(continued)

Reader 1: **Fall**

I am the wind the witches ride,
the wind of fall.
When you trick-or-treat,
crunching leaves beneath your feet,
then I'll go haunting, too—
rattling the windows
when you knock on the door,
crackling bare branches of the trees,
hissing at the jack-o'-lantern's candle.
HISSSS!

Reader 2: **Winter**

I am the wind of winter.
Whip! Wallop! Whoosh!
Bundle up when you hear me huffle.
I'll nip your nose.
I'll bite your toes.
I howl and blow
and herd the snow.
Whip! Wallop! Whoosh!

Partner Poems for Building Fluency   Scholastic Teaching Resources

The Colors

The world around us is full of colors. If they could talk, what might they tell us? Through a variety of images, this poem lets students see everyday colors in a whole new way.

Building Fluency With the Poem

◌ Model and Discuss

After reading the poem, ask: "What is your favorite color? Did the poem make you see this color differently?" Then do a modeled reading, pausing between each stanza and emphasizing the color labels to signal the new hue. Read the first stanza in a rhythmic way, stressing its rhyme. Then emphasize the descriptive qualities of the free verse, using an expressive voice to highlight vivid language. Explain: "The first stanza of this poem rhymes. The stanzas about each color do not and the rhythm does not have a regular pattern. This is called free verse. Notice the descriptive language used to talk about each color: For instance, green is *the cool one* while red is an *attention getter*. I use a soothing voice to describe green, and an attention-getting voice to describe red. Reading with expression helps listeners form a picture in their mind."

◌ Whole-Group Practice

For this piece, you may want to focus on one or two stanzas a day before bringing it all together. You can focus on different skills for each color, such as dialogue in the Red stanza and alliteration (*brief blaze*) in the Orange verse. Have the class read each stanza chorally, pointing out descriptive language as you go.

◌ Partner Practice

Have partners practice the poem section by section (two stanzas at a time, each student taking the role of one color). Then students can put the whole poem together, dividing it as indicated (Reader 1 and Reader 2).

Vocabulary

You may wish to preview the following words from the poem:

◌ chalice ◌ illusion

◌ delphinium ◌ nectar

◌ ermine

Extension Activity

Have students choose a favorite color and without naming the color, have them write clues that describe it. Use prompts such as: "What feelings does this color give you? Where do you see it? What might it say?" They can use personification and have the color speak with a human voice. For example: *I am the color of a cat's nose, a cuddly piglet, or even a carnation. I'm soft and warm, but you might also see me on your cheeks if the wind is cold!* Post the descriptions on a bulletin board and provide the class with crayons. As they read each poem, students can mark the page with the color they think it's about. Together, see how readers interpreted each piece. Then ask the author to reveal the color! (In this case, pink.)

The Colors

Readers 1 & 2:

If colors on a color wheel
could tell us
what they think or feel
Can you imagine
what they'd say?
Maybe they might
speak this way:

Reader 1:

Green:
I'm the beginning
of something new.
I am the spring thing,
The cool one.
I green the grass
          and leaf
                the trees.
          I dress the frogs.

Reader 2:

Red:
I'm an attention getter.
I say, "Look at me!"
Red is what you see
when a fire engine streaks
down the street.
I say, "Look!
The strawberries are ripe."
I'm the signal that means
it's time to pick a tomato.
It's been said
that angry people see red.
I don't know about that.
But who can think of valentines
without seeing me?

(continued)

Partner Poems for Building Fluency   Scholastic Teaching Resources   Poem copyright © 2007 by Bobbi Katz.

Reader 1:

Yellow:
Everyone chooses
a yellow crayon
to color the distant sun.
But remember,
I am not just the center
of the solar system.
You'll find the white petals
of every daisy
revolve around me, too.

Reader 2:

Blue:
Is there really so much of me?
Am I often an illusion, actually?
I seem to be the color of sky,
and a blue sky can make a blue sea.
It's certain that I'm the color of
bluebells,
delphinium,
chicory,
forget-me-nots…
And, of course, blue eyes.

Reader 1:

Orange:
Yes, sometime in July you might see
a brief blaze of orange flowers
race across a field.
A few days later they seem to disappear,
By October those same blossoms
have been recycled
into plump orange pumpkins.
They look no more like flowers
than butterflies look like caterpillars.
But to know
the real meaning of orange,
find the fruit
for which I'm named...
Peel away its zesty skin.
Smell.
Taste.
Know me at my best.

Reader 2:

Purple:
Once upon a time,
kings in purple velvet robes
trimmed with white ermine
drank purple nectar
from a jeweled cup
called a chalice.
Kings are few these days,
but I still have fans.
Starting young,
they always choose "grape"
if the subject is juice
or Popsicles.
If the subject is flowers,
they admire stately iris
and sweet-smelling lilac.
When they're lucky,
they might find wild violets—
enough to pick a bunch
to bring home!

Partner Poems for Building Fluency Scholastic Teaching Resources

Presidential Tailor Talk

George Washington and Abraham Lincoln were two great presidents. They were also two very different men who lived in different times. In this imaginative and informative biography in rhyme, voices of the two presidents' tailors give students a new way to think about American history!

Building Fluency With the Poem

Model and Discuss

Start by eliciting students' prior knowledge of the two presidents, and review challenging vocabulary. Explain that before sewing machines were invented, people did not buy their clothes in stores. Clothes were sewn at home. Some people had personal tailors, who made their clothing to order. Then read the poem and check comprehension by asking: "Who is telling us about each president? What do the tailors teach us about these men?" In your modeled reading, slow down on important vocabulary words and use your voice to emphasize the contrasts between Washington and Lincoln. Explain: "For a poem like this one, it's especially important to study the words before reading it aloud. If I'm not sure what a word means or how it's pronounced, I look it up in the dictionary. This way, when it's time to read, I know how to say words like *waistcoat, homespun,* and *serge* smoothly and with expression. Comparisons and contrasts are also very important in this poem. I emphasize phrases that tell how the two men are alike and different."

Whole-Group Practice

Go over pronunciation of difficult words and answer any questions students may have about their definitions. Then do a line-by-line echo reading of the poem, having students repeat after you. You might also like to have students paraphrase each line, using their own words to reinforce comprehension.

Partner Practice

Before reading, have partners circle any words they are still unsure of and look them up. Also have students highlight words and phrases that show contrast, encouraging them to emphasize these when reading aloud.

Vocabulary

You may wish to preview the following words from the poem:

- bankrupt
- economies
- humanity
- precedent

Extension Activity

Use the piece as a jumping-off point for practice with biographical descriptions. Have partners choose two people they admire for different reasons. They can brainstorm ideas by dividing a sheet of paper in half and listing significant qualities of each person. Then have partners use the prewriting organizer to write a compare-contrast paragraph about the two people. Let students read aloud their work to the group.

Presidential Tailor Talk

Readers 1 & 2:

Two presidents lived years apart.
Both served the nation well.
If we could hear their tailors talk,
what tales might tailors tell?

Reader 1 (George Washington's Tailor):

He was a tall young gentleman.
Sat well upon a horse.
He welcomed every chance to dance,
which ladies liked, of course.
But even though his years were few,
his demands were…many.
He specified each dart, each hem.
Economies?
Not any!

Reader 2 (Abraham Lincoln's Tailor):

A tall and rugged farm boy,
Abe worked in Offutt's store,
until the store went bankrupt
and his job there was no more.
With a part-time post as postmaster,
plus a part-time post surveying,
Abe made a patchwork living
picking up odd jobs like haying.
When he ran for the Assembly,
that's when he came to me,
I made him a homespun suit
as plain as it could be.
He didn't seem to care a jot
if it fit just right or not.
I was glad to vote for him.
All four times I helped him win!

(continued)

Partner Poems for Building Fluency   Scholastic Teaching Resources   Poem copyright © 2007 by Bobbi Katz.

Reader 1 (General George Washington's Tailor):

He wants a waistcoat of blue wool
with pleats on either side
and gold braid on the shoulders—
not quite two inches wide.
He needs a cape for winter
to keep out wind and chill,
and what the general wants he'll get.
Yes, I'll see that he will.
He's leading our brave soldiers
and doesn't wish a cent,
yet he still cares what he's wearing,
while living in a tent.
When our lads see their general
it will give them heart
to see he's costumed perfectly
to play the general's part.

(continued)

Reader 2 (President Abraham Lincoln's Tailor):

He's the tallest man in Springfield.
I feel honored I can say
I cut black serge for all his suits
before he went away.
When he was elected
to be the president,
I thought that he might change his style—
more like a fancy gent.
But no, he kept his stovepipe hat,
which added to his height.
You couldn't miss him in a crowd.
He was a striking sight.
No tailor will get rich from him.
He lacks all vanity.
Yet the pattern of his spirit
cloaks all humanity.

Reader 1 (President George Washington's Tailor):

There wasn't any precedent.
There'd never been a president!
There were no rules for such a thing.
Should a president dress like a king?
Now he's elected. Yes, that's true,
and who comes calling? Me and you!
Just whom would we expect to see—
some farmer—or real royalty?
The president, I'm pleased to say,
dresses in the royal way.
He'll greet guests without exception,
formally, at a reception.